I

THE FIRST THIRTEEN YEARS

by

GEORGE J. SAITER ED.D.

Edited by

Norma J. Saiter MA

How The "George Saiter School of Excellence" Began

First Edition published by
GEONOR Publishing Co 5/2015
Fort Morgan, Co.

GEONOR
Publishing
Company
Fort Morgan, CO

ISBN - 978-0-9844377-6-4

Printed in the United states of America

Bill Brown

This book is dedicated to

William (Bill) Brown.

Bill worked by my side the entire
First Thirteen Years.
Without him
there would not be a
"George Saiter
School of Excellence"
today.
I treasure his friendship.

Table of Contents:
The First Thirteen Years

PROLOGUE

June 22, 2013

My family and I were vacationing near Banff, Canada when I received a phone call from, my longtime friend, William (Bill) Brown of Colorado Springs. Bill was currently on the Board of Directors for The NEED Foundation. He apprised me of the large "Best Grant" to be used for remodeling the Gorman Junior High school building as the new headquarters for the Pikes Peak BOCES and the new home of what was once known as NEED School (New Emotional Educational Development).

Brown said the dedication of the building would be August 1, 2013 and asked me if I would be willing to come to Colorado Springs and speak at the opening. I said I would be thrilled to speak at the opening. A month later I received an invitation to attend the "Ribbon Cutting Ceremony and Open House for Pikes Peak BOCES and the George Saiter School of Excellence."

I was overwhelmed. What greater tribute could an educator receive? This started me to thinking back almost forty years to the battles, struggles, and successes of the early days of NEED. As though it were yesterday, the faces of staff and children began to appear in my mind. A subtle smile slowly blossomed until it consumed my whole face.

CHAPTER ONE

THE BIRTH OF A DREAM

1974-1977

The "George Saiter School of Excellence" did not just happen. Its roots lie in a program called "NEED." The plan to start a school for "troubled kids" was dreamed up, nurtured, and painfully developed over forty years ago during the 1970's. Dr. George Saiter, the dreamer, labored long hours, endured multiple disappointments and successes during those formative years. As soon as one obstacle was deflected, another would pop up even more menacing than the last. It was a constant battle to keep the flame alive. This story relates the struggles of the first dozen years. There were many more, but these were the major episodes. Dedicated staff continued to deliver quality education and treatment to students and families while George struggled with the many obstacles. Controversy continuously swirled around the program and often threatened its very existence.

There seemed to be a large, wicked dragon looking down from above that would intermittently shower them with its fiery breath and attempt to blow out the flickering flame.

George was helped in his quest by a host of dedicated staff, school superintendents, supervisors, and especially, Bill Brown. We must also include Dr. Goodwin who restarted the idea after the BOCES Board killed it, and Wayne Hoeben, a longtime friend. Hoeben "pulled our bacon out of the fire" when city inspectors threatened to put a halt to our plans.

When George joined the Pikes Peak BOCES in 1974 they served 21 school districts. The urban districts were getting under way with the new federally mandated Special Education programs, but the smaller districts didn't have a clue as to what they needed to do. The larger urban districts included Air Academy, Harrison, Widefield, and Fountain. The intermediate size school districts were Manitou Springs, Cheyenne Mountain, Palmer Lake, Lewis Palmer, and Falcon. The small districts were Cripple Creek and Woodland Park in the mountains and scattered over the plains east of Colorado Springs were Peyton, Calhan, Simla, Elbert, Elizabeth, Kiowa, Ellicott, Edison, Hanover, and Miami Yoder.

Three psychologists served 21 school districts. One psychologist served Air Academy, and the other 20 districts were divided between George and Ouida Neal. Neal was the first psychologist hired by the BOCES after it's inception. The BOCES had one special education teacher to serve the school districts of Peyton, Calhan, Simla, Elbert, Elizabeth, Kiowa, Ellicott, Edison, Hanover, and Miami Yoder out on the plains east of Colorado Springs. Emily Bissel visited each school one day every two weeks. That could be called a *minimal* Special Education Program, to say the least.

Norma Bristow moved from Greeley to Colorado Springs in December of 1974 and became the second full time special education teacher for the plains schools. She was assigned to the Peyton School District. The next year she was moved to Falcon School District. Falcon consisted of one school building that housed first through twelfth grades.

School districts with more than 4500 students, by state

law, could form their own special education program. Those districts with less than 4500 students were required to join a BOCES. Air Academy, Widefield, Harrison, and Fountain soon departed from the BOCES and formed their own units. They later rejoined the BOCES as associate members.

Dr. Abbot, BOCES Director, assigned George to supervise the educational programs in the area residential programs and serve as School Psychologist for a number of BOCES districts. These residential programs needed a state certified educational program to fulfill legal requirements. Each of them requested this service from the BOCES. George assumed the role of supervising and hiring the teachers and aides at Brady Psychiatric Hospital, Brockhurst Boys Ranch, (a nonprofit program for troubled children from several states), Zebulon Pike Detention Center, (El Paso County's center for teenagers who were arrested and incarcerated for a short time), and The Youth Treatment Center, (a private residential program for troubled children). He also supervised a classroom of disruptive elementary students housed at Wilson school.

Children were sent to these residential programs because they were so disruptive they could not function in the home or in school.

The programs were very expensive. Funding was provided by the parents, if they could afford it, Departments of Social Services, or insurances. The best insurance program was CHAMPUS for active or retired Military personnel. There were about twenty five special education teachers and aides scattered over the four programs.

George's referrals from BOCES districts slowly evolved into mainly disruptive students. If he was not successful in recommending procedures to deal with the youngsters in the regular school he would seek placement in one of the programs he supervised. This was fine for wealthy parents, military families, and those with good health insurance. If no funding sources were available, he would turn to the El Paso Department of Social Services. It was extremely difficult to get approval from the county to treat a disruptive student unless he had committed a crime. Sadly enough, many were in trouble with the law.

In spite of these resources, a number of problem students were impossible to fund and place. Many disruptive students were simply expelled from school and the parents were left to cope with them on their own. This situation was troubling to George. Several years later revised State and Federal laws forbade schools from expelling troubled students unless they placed them in alternative programs.

Dr. Ed Abbot resigned from the BOCES in 1976, and Dr. Goodwin was hired to replaced him. George continued his work with troubled children and the treatment programs. Due to the intensity of the problems, he became well known to most of the superintendents. More than one superintendent or principal related to George how much extra time he had after a disruptive child had been moved to a treatment program.

George began preparing extensive reports on each case and forwarded them to Dr. Goodwin. Each time he had a case for which he was unable to find placement he ended the report with, "We need to develop our own program." Each time, Dr. Goodwin told him there was no way the Board or the Superintendents would fund such a program.

George foresaw a day treatment school where disruptive students would be provided adaptive education and therapy. Their parents would also receive therapy and be taught strategies for dealing with their youngsters.

George began to campaign with district superintendents

for a day treatment program of their own. The idea was slow to catch fire. There was a standoff between the school districts and El Paso County Department Social Services. The schools thought DSS should take care of disruptive youngsters that could not be managed in the regular classroom, and DSS thought the schools should provide for them. The children and their families were caught in the middle with no help from either side.

There was also a big controversy within special education about which disruptive students were eligible for special education services. Behavior so disruptive they could not be tolerated in a classroom was not enough. The Colorado State Department Education decreed a student must have a recognizable psychiatric mental health diagnosis, such as schizophrenia, to be served in special education. Otherwise, they were simply behavior disordered and were not eligible for special education services. They could be expelled from school and the district had no responsibility for their education.

George was critical of the state and schools that took care of their problem by delegating the student to the streets. Expelled students often fell in with wrong companions and committed crimes.

A number of parents came to George for help after their child was expelled from school. Their only recourse was to declare to DSS, in court, they could no longer manage their child and relinquish their parental rights. Then, DSS had the problem. Most parents were reluctant to take this step.

Some children were accepted by DSS and put in residential treatment when the child could have stayed in his home with day treatment and family guidance. Day treatment would be much less costly than residential treatment. This help would bolster the parents and the child. George thought it was a joint responsibility of the schools and DSS to solve the problem.

Dr. Goodwin finally acquiesced in February 1978. George had again gone to Dr. Goodwin's office to plead for a program for troubled youngsters. George did not like these confrontations because Goodwin often got angry, but George was on a crusade. Goodwin finally told George to develop a budget for a program to present to the March board meeting. He said the board would surely turn it down, but to go ahead and try. George knew Goodwin agreed mostly to get rid of his badgering, but that did not matter. He had a "go ahead."

George was elated. He decided to propose two classrooms of ten students each. He would need two special education teachers, two teacher aides and a social worker. He developed a budget to include salaries, books, classroom supplies, and cost of housing. The budget, if accepted, would cost $35 per student day. This would be a yearly cost of $6300. Schools were budgeting about $2500 per student year at the time. George knew the cost would be troublesome so he presented only a daily cost. He would leave it up to the board members to do the math.

Next, he needed a name. He sat down with Norma, his new wife, across the kitchen table to discuss his project. Most treatment programs at the time had the word treatment in their name. He thought this was demeaning to the students. George had visited a fledgling program in Denver for troubled youngsters. Their program was called NEAT, (New Educational and Attitude Treatment.) He wanted an acronym that would be easy to remember. Norma and George tossed around different names and finally agreed on NEED, New Educational Emotional Development.

George presented the proposal to the BOCES superintendents at their monthly meeting on the first Tuesday of March 1978. There were many questions. Most of the BOCES schools experienced problems with disruptive students. Some superintendents felt the children chose to act that way. Other superintendents agreed with George that there were internal and external forces influencing the disruptive behavior. A majority of the superintendents voted to forward the proposal to the BOCES Governing Board at their next meeting.

The BOCES board was made up of one school board member from each member and associate member school. They met on the second Tuesday of each month. George carefully described in detail the problem the proposal was designed to mitigate. He described the facilities in the community that serve troubled children. He compared his proposed cost to community residential facilities. He explained that only those families who were well off, or had good insurance, could afford the cost. There were unmet needs in the community. The proposal would provide for these unmet needs. George visioned a program that would not only provide education, but also treatment for the child and guidance for the whole family. The main selling point was that it would cost a district nothing unless they chose to send a child to the program.

Board members asked many questions but did not question the cost. After much discussion, a motion was made to approve the proposal. It passed with a unanimous vote. NEED was on the way. The board directed George to hire staff, buy supplies, and find a location for the program. George was elated. Goodwin was extremely surprised, but pleased that the board accepted George's proposal. Goodwin didn't know it at the time but NEED would eventually grow into the main source of revenue for the BOCES.

The El Paso Community College had just vacated six buildings and moved to a new campus. One of the vacant buildings was available at a ridiculously low cost. George developed a proposal to buy the building for presentation to the board.

George was in his office a few days later when he received

a call from the Special Education Director of Air Academy. He had just interviewed a social worker from Milwaukee who was planning to move to Colorado Springs. There was no vacancy for Brown in Air Academy, but he asked George if he would give the social worker a courtesy interview. George wasn't in a position to interview staff yet, but he would provide the favor for his friend.

Bill Brown

Bill Brown would only be in town today and would head back home tomorrow. Brown showed up promptly at 3:30 that afternoon. He had impressive credentials. George liked Brown and felt he should try to hire him while he was available. He needed permission from Goodwin before he could make a commitment. They shook hands and promised to talk again. Bill left for home.

The next day, with Goodwin's approval, George called Wanda, Bill's wife, in Milwaukee. He had left his home number. George introduced himself to Wanda and informed her there was a spot in NEED for Bill.

This was a great hire. He stayed with NEED until he retired. Bill was a loyal employee who gave strength to the program. He was the one who put George's ideas into operation.

George was excited about the board meeting the second Tuesday of April, but the first of many disasters was about to strike. George briefed the board on the progress so far and the proposed building purchase.

There was a lull in the conversation.

The dragon opened his huge mouth and spewed his flame.

One of the board members spoke up. "This is a lot of money. It is more than we spend on GOOD kids! I make a motion to scrap the whole project." George was devastated. She had voted for it last month. He sat in bewilderment as each board member voted to approve the motion. All of his hard work was "down the drain."

The worst part was Brown. He had already quit his job in Milwaukie and was busy packing to move to Colorado Springs. George could not bring himself to make the call. He somehow subconsciously still had hope. He chose to "drag his feet." Maybe he could find another spot for Brown somewhere in the area.

George's long campaign still seemed to have legs. Goodwin had seen the interest of some superintendents in the proposal. So he decided to help. He contacted four superintendents who had favored the idea to discuss some way to save the program. Dr. Gary Miller of Manitou Springs, Dr. Ray Kilmer of Lewis Palmer, Wayne Bricker of Harrison, and John Asbury of Air Academy met with Goodwin. There was much conversation on solutions. They finally decided, as a group, to guarantee the tuition of fifteen students for one year even though they might not use the slots. This would cost the other districts nothing. There would be no reason to turn it down.

This new proposal was presented to the BOCES board at their next meeting. The board unanimously approved the pilot program, but the new building was out. George would have to find somewhere else to house the two classrooms.

George was back in business. Bill had a job again. This was only the first of many disasters that would threaten the existence of NEED during the next ten years. George's resolve and resources would be tested to their limits time and again.

The dragon was waiting for him in the shadows.

George's second impressive hire was Sheila Jobes. She was hired as one of the two original NEED teachers. Sheila had student taught with Norma Bristow. Norma said she was the best student teacher she had ever taught. She thought Sheila possessed great insights and expertise.

Sheila had taken a position in a school in Wisconsin the first year out of college. It turned out to be a disaster. She confided in Norma that her year was so bad she was going to quit education. This would be her last year. Norma told George of this outstanding teacher and campaigned for her.

After George received the final approval for NEED, he

Sheila Jobes

had a long phone conversation with Sheila. He had been acquainted with her while she lived in Greeley. He told her he thought she belonged in education and offered her a job. She was reluctant. She had already made up her mind to find another profession. George insisted until she finally said she would think about it.

A week later she called to say she would try it for one year. What a gift George brought to the community.

Sheila stayed with NEED for two years then moved to other positions in the BOCES. She later became an outstanding Special Education Director for The Fountain

School District. After retiring from Fountain, she spent several years with the Colorado Department of Education. In 2013 she had a program and building in Fountain, Colorado named after her.

Other hires were not successful. There was a great turn over in staff the first five years. Slowly, the staff began to stabilize. Only a few teachers are capable of working with disruptive, troubled students day after day. George was able to attract and keep a number of strong solid staff during his 13 year infatuation with NEED. When he retired seventy percent of the staff had been with him five or more years. Some remained with NEED until their retirement.

George now had staff and it was time to attend to the details. He must develop a curriculum, buy books, determine schedules, and dozens of other details required to start a new school. Several trips to the Military Surplus Store supplied metal desks for the teachers and Bill. George decided to use the Widefield School schedule. The home schools would transport the students to and from NEED. He made an appointment with the Curriculum Director at Manitou Springs whom he highly respected. Together, they planned a curriculum and ordered books. This worked out well because when he needed an extra book he could borrow one from Manitou Springs. The details kept him busy well into the summer, but George was used to working on his own time. If his yearly salary at BOCES had been divided by the hours he worked he probably would have been earning below the minimum hourly wage.

CHAPTER TWO

WILSON ELEMENTARY SCHOOL

1978-1980

NEED officially began in September, 1978 with six students, one social worker, two teachers, and two classroom aides. Students were accepted from seventh through twelfth grades. An elementary program would have to wait until later years.

The new NEED program was to be housed in two classrooms across from Dr. Goodwin's office at BOCES located in the vacated Wilson Elementary School building in Widefield. Bill's office would be in a classroom used for storage and the building copy machine. It was impossible for him to have a confidential conversation with a student. Bill had a job, but he would have to wait for an office upgrade. During the next two years the program slowly grew to three classrooms and additional staff.

Over the years, referrals were rarely a problem. The two continuing problems were funding and lodging. Everyone wanted the service. No one wanted to pay for it. Lodging for NEED would continue to be a problem until they could own a building of their own. Everyone agreed it was a worthwhile program but "not in my back yard with my money."

Troubled youngsters have prolific vocabularies of foul language and freely use this vocabulary to express their feelings. Mother becomes the first part of a hyphenated word. It was not uncommon for an angry student to burst into the hall outside Goodwin's office and shout at the top of his voice, "THIS @###&**! ###%&** PLACE SUCKS!" Goodwin's neck hairs would stand on end. He was an old time superintendent who believed in strong discipline. His first impulse was to grab the student by the scruff of the neck and eject him from school. He fought that urge and allowed NEED staff do their job, but he never got used to it.

George enjoyed the students. He could tolerate the bad times because when they were mellow they were a delight. One rainy night the doorbell rang at George's home. Four of his students appeared at the door soaked to the skin. They had been up town in Colorado Springs and couldn't make it home before the rain. He brought them in to dry their clothes. They were delightful to talk with. Where one sat on one of his wooden chairs the stains remain today. After they dried out he took them home.

A year later one of those nighttime visitors was convicted of a felony and sent to prison. Years later another was convicted of auto manslaughter and sent to prison.

Not all students were successful. George followed most

of his former students after they graduated from NEED. He determined NEED was able to turn around three out of five students who completed the program. They became tax payers instead of tax takers.

One girl in the program diagnosed with schizophrenic symptoms seemed to be mirroring her schizophrenic mother's behavior rather than actually being clinically schizophrenic. Her father came to George one day begging him to find a place for his girl away from her mother. He was afraid his girl would develop the disorder just from being around her mother. George consulted other mental health workers and his staff and they agreed that was a possibility. She needed to be separated from her mother until she grew emotionally stronger.

George made an appointment with DSS supervisors and asked what they could do for the situation. They had no solution. The girl did not fit the guidelines for help, and they were not flexible enough to try to find a solution. He tried every avenue he could think of with no help. When the father came to his office in tears for the third time, George told him his daughter could live with him and his wife for a while.

This was a surprise to George's new wife, Norma, because he had failed to include her in the decision. However, she was a good sport and went along with the arrangement. George and Norma had the girl in their home for almost a year and treated her as their own. She spent each weekend with her family. When she came back each Sunday evening she acted crazy. This lasted for about a day, then she became normal again. She continued in NEED during this time. There were some problems since she would often exploit the fact she was living with the director, but these problems were worked out.

After about ten months the girl seemed stable enough to return home for a trial. The trial turned into full time at home.

She had become emotionally strong enough to withstand the influences of her mother. George's decision to keep the teenager in his home was never popular with his staff, but he felt he and Norma helped the girl and that made it worthwhile.

Goodwin tolerated NEED students for two years. He then told George he must take his program elsewhere. In Dr. Goodwin's defense, he was often embarrassed by student tirades when he had visitors in his office. After all what do you say to a visitor when a teenager is shouting obscenities in the hall outside your office?

CHAPTER - THREE

ROCKY MOUNTAIN REHAB BUILDING

1980-1982

George discovered there was a vacant wing available in the Rocky Mountain Rehab building on East Yampa St. It had housed a program for intellectually challenged children who were excluded from public schools. Previous laws allowed schools to exclude children with IQs of 50 or lower. The new federal law for children with disabilities declared all children must be cared for by the public schools. The BOCES took over the program one year before. George had helped move and develop this program at Wilson School.

George was able to secure a lease on the vacant wing. NEED thrived. With the extra space, they were able to take all the referrals they received. (He believed the program should be flexible enough to accept all referrals from member districts.)

Student population grew from 20 to over fifty in a few months. Two more classroom teachers and an art teacher were added. A kiln was installed in the art room. Each student received art therapy every day. Each teacher had an aide. Studies were departmentalized. Students rotated through three classrooms and the art class.

Some students could not handle these hourly changes of rooms and teachers. They needed more structure. To meet this need George hired a teacher and an aide for a self-contained classroom within the program.

Two social workers, a psychologist, and a part-time speech therapist were added. Ted Grubb was the first psychologist hired to exclusively serve NEED students.

George was pleased with the program as it matured and could provide additional services. The numbers of students in the program justified the staff. The clinical staff per student ratio was a continuing disagreement between Goodwin and George. However, George stubbornly held the line at ten students per therapist. Occasionally, this number was temporarily exceeded. When this happened, George took some cases or hired a new therapist.

George kept a close eye on costs so he never exceeded the budgeted student per day cost. Some school districts would use the program, then decide the cost was too high and pull their students out, only to change their minds when they could not handle the problem students or find less costly alternatives. This provided great fluctuations in the student population. Student populations were greatly reduced when school started in the fall. There was also a lively turnover of staff at the end of each year. George would not fill the vacated slots at the start of each school year until the numbers of students justified the hires. The student population usually increased to full capacity by November each year.

As the program grew, George felt overloaded. Even though NEED had grown considerably he was still responsible for the four residential educational programs and psychological referrals from the districts. He was lucky to spend half time at NEED due to his other duties. The complexity of the treatment and educational components of NEED required closer supervision, but he was unable to convince his supervisor. He needed to reorganize the program to improve supervision and the delivery of services. George could not offer increased salaries, but he proceeded to develop supervisory positions. He hoped that eventually these positions would merit additional pay for the increased responsibilities.

He made Brown the Clinical Director. Bill would have direct supervision and training of all clinical staff. He planned to elevate one teacher to a Head Teacher position to oversee the educational program, attend to substitutes, and attend all referral staffing. He had attended all referral staffing up to this time.

He conferred with Goodwin on the Head Teacher appointment since it would require hiring another classroom teacher. After his conversation with Goodwin, George assumed he had approval for the change. He proceeded with the promotion and the new hire. He received a delayed letter in the mail several days later from Goodwin instructing him not to make the change. He never knew why Goodwin chose to send a letter instead of picking up the phone.

George had a dilemma. He had already promoted Bud Benusa to Head Teacher and hired the replacement teacher. George gave it much anguished thought. He finally decided to ignore the letter and act as though it never existed. He proceeded to send the contract for the additional teacher through the regular channels for approval. Goodwin approved the contract without comment. Neither Goodwin nor George ever mentioned the letter to each other.

Ten children were assigned to each clinical staff member. They were to provide therapy for the student and guidance for his family. They would also accompany the student to judicial hearings if the child was involved with the law. They were to liaison with all and any community agencies involved with the child. George believed NEED should be available to help the parents 24/7. One treatment staff member was assigned each week to be available 24 hours per day and weekends for family emergencies. These were all tasks George had done in the past so he was relieved of much of his load.

He also shed some of his outside of NEED duties. The Youth Treatment Center folded, and Shelia Jobes took over supervision of Brockhurst Boys Ranch. This greatly relieved his load and stress, but other duties always seemed to fill his time.

In the spring of 1983, the El Paso Placement Alternatives Committee approved NEED for the placement of adolescents who were in danger of being removed from their home and placed in residential treatment programs. For the first time a community agency was committed to join with the schools to help fund the services provided by NEED. This would be a huge savings for the county for any child NEED could keep in the home was much less costly than residential treatment.

The Rocky Mountain Rehab building proved not to be a good fit for NEED because the owner of the building, the non-profit Rocky Mountain Rehab Foundation, was located in the main part of the building. Student incidents strained the relationship. One of these incidents was when one or more NEED students spray painted the building and cut down a medium sized tree in the courtyard during the night. The building owners were incensed. George, with the help of Brown, scrubbed the walls over and over until the paint dimmed enough to be acceptable. George, out of his own funds, bought a replacement fifteen-foot tree and they planted it where the original one was cut down. Tension continued to build between RMRF and NEED.

The "last straw" occurred when one of the students told a used car salesman he was going to buy a car and wanted to try one out. He then drove around the Rocky Mountain Rehab building twice before plowing into a couple of cars owned by RMR employees. One of the cars was a vintage Bug. George determined the student was not hurt, informed the parents, and then went to the property owner's office to try to make amends. He had two very angry people, the car owners and the landlord. George was told, in no uncertain terms, to take his NEED program and go away. "Go somewhere else, any place but here." He was given until the end of the school year to vacate. NEED had not been a good neighbor.

George was out on the street again. However, he had survived another two years. He could not really blame them. These two incidents were just two of many clashes between his students and the "other" world.

Moving the school was difficult since he could not afford movers. George moved the program each time with the help of any volunteers he could find, (usually Brown and his family), and a U-Haul or borrowed truck.

CHAPTER - FOUR

THE BLAIR BUILDING

1982 - 1984

George looked at every location in Colorado Springs that he could afford and would hold the program. He found locations, but the owners either would not rent to him or the neighbors were hostile. Nobody liked his kids the way he did.

One day he saw an article in the newspaper. Blair Business College was closing its doors. He wondered if the building on North Farragut might be available for lease. The Blair Building was a two-story building with more than enough room for the program. It was situated in a residential area across the street from a city park. He located the owner. It was available.

George was successful in negotiating a lease at his price since no one else was bidding on the building. NEED again had a home. For the first time, they had no "in-building" neighbors to present problems. They would have a whole building to themselves with room to grow. Their neighbor problems were over. Not true, as we will see.

During the summer, George rented a truck, and, with the help of volunteers (Bill, his family and some staff members), moved NEED for the second time. He had a great building, but no furniture. There were not even towel dispensers in the bathrooms. A substantial amount of George's personal funds went into equipment. There was no money in the budget for fixtures or furniture. He had a few student and teacher's desks from Wilson elementary. (Student desks went with the lease at the last building.) He approached member schools for any surplus furniture. He received a lot of surplus furniture from Colorado Springs District 11. The District 11 Building Supervisor had a son in the program and he was very helpful. George finally gathered enough furniture and equipment together to start school.

NEED opened for the 1982/83 school year in the Blair building on North Farragut. NEED continued to flourish with periodic episodes that threatened to completely destroy it.

The building was spacious with more room than the program could use. The usual low student count prevailed as the school year started but referrals began to flood in. As the student count increased, George added the necessary staff.

The typical NEED teacher constantly lived with extreme stress. The classroom seemed to be constantly on the edge of blowing up. It required gifted classroom management skills. Most teachers could not handle the stress. However, experienced teachers were plentiful in the area due to the large military population. Many military wives were certified teachers. George was able to hire certified teachers as classroom aides. He hired several excellent teachers that first year in the Blair building. Two of them, Jane Briggs and Linda Bowles, were still with NEED when he retired. He added a certified nurse with counseling experience and a new secretary. The new secretary, Carol Gardner, was a special find. She was still with NEED when George retired and continued until she retired.

The school year 1984/85 brought more strain to George's life. There were always rumors about Colorado Springs District 11 starting its own program and pulling their students out. This was a worry since, without the district 11 students, it would be difficult to pay the rent on the building.

Two districts did just that at the beginning of the year. Colorado Springs School District #11 and Widefield School District #3 developed intensive care programs of their own to serve the needs of students they had been sending to NEED. This event eliminated approximately 50 percent of the NEED student population, and required a reduction in NEED staff. Several NEED staff had quit the end of the preceding school year so George did not have to lay anyone off. He just adjusted the remaining staff to the smaller student number. This condition did not last long.

As the year progressed, referrals continued to multiply. Even District #11 and #3 again began to send students they couldn't handle in their new programs.

A number of area schools went to the middle school concept which included 6th grade so NEED began accepting sixth grade students for the first time. Amazingly, staff and student population was back to former levels by the middle of the school year.

George thought it might be easier to solicit donations as a non-profit organization. Therefore, his next project was the development of a non-profit foundation. He and Norma socialized with an attorney, Jeff Zelmanow, and his wife.

The attorney's wife was a special education teacher at Falcon School District. George talked with Zelmanow about the possibility of providing some pro-bono time. Jeff was glad to do it. Together they developed a non-profit organization. The NEED Foundation, Inc. was certified by the state of Colorado in September, 1985. The NEED Foundation, Inc. became vital in later years to buy and hold buildings to house NEED.

George was in blissful ignorance of a swelling unrest in the neighborhood. His first hint of unrest came when he received a summons from the city of Colorado Springs.

He was summoned to attend a hearing scheduled to determine if NEED was a nuisance in the neighborhood and should be closed. All the neighbors had signed the petition, even those blocks away. Need had become well known in the area.

About the same time as the summons, one of the students confided to George that one of his classmates (I'll call him Ned) had a gun in school! This was the first and last time a gun was found at school during George's time as director. (There were episodes of knives, but this was the only gun incident.) George called the police. George thought of the impending hearing before city council and shivered at the possible consequences of this incident.

George informed Brown about the situation and told him he would take charge of the classroom. He wanted to get the teacher out of harm's way immediately. He would send the teacher out of the room on the ruse of a phone call. Brown would meet her in the hall and apprise her of the situation then return to the office to await the police. Brown was to put the officer in George's office, then come to the classroom and let him know the police had arrived. When Brown showed up at the classroom door George asked Ned to come with him to his office. Ned complied without comment. He exhibited no apparent concern about going with George. The teacher returned to take control of the classroom.

George walked into his office with Ned. Ned seemed mildly surprised to see two policemen. George calmly told Ned he had information he had a gun on him. To George's dismay, Ned pulled TWO loaded silver plated pistols from his pocket and handed them to him. George just stood there for a moment somewhat shocked by the two pistols in his hands and the ease at which Ned surrendered them.

Ned was a good student who never caused trouble. George would never have suspected him of bringing guns to school. George handed the two pistols to one of the officers and they placed Ned under arrest.

Ned was extremely apologetic. The guns belonged to his father. Ned said he never planned to use them. He just wanted to feel macho, and had brought them to school to impress the other students. He certainly achieved this goal as well as surprising the whole NEED staff. The officers took Ned away and George never saw him again or heard what happened to him.

The call had gone out over the police radio system. The press picked up the call. When the police left the school a bevy of reporters was clustered outside. The last thing George wanted was to have this incident blown up in the newspaper. His experience with reporters had been negative. They never seemed to report what George had said. The conversation was always twisted to make a better story. George told Brown to talk with the reporters. That way George could always deny whatever was reported.

The neighbors became even more aggravated and frightened when they read about the gun incident in the newspaper.

The day of the hearing George's attorney friend, Zelmanow, planned to be at the meeting to advise him. When George arrived the hearing room was packed. He found a seat down front and watched the committee take their seats. George was nervous. If he was kicked out of the Blair Building it could be the end of NEED. The chairperson struck the gavel and announced the reason for the meeting.

The committee would determine if NEED was a threat and a nuisance and/or a danger to the neighborhood, and if so, should the council recommend it be closed. The chairperson asked those in the audience who wanted to testify against NEED to raise their hands. George looked over his shoulder. As nearly as he could count, over 100 persons raised their hands. When the chairperson asked for the hands of those who would testify for NEED, George was the lone responder. He was out numbered to the max.

Zelmanow had not arrived.

George was nervous.

Zelmanow arrived twenty minutes later. This made George feel better. There was comfort in numbers even if the number was only two. Person after person walked to the podium to testify against the program.

They asked George accusatory questions.

"Isn't it true that senior citizens are most often the victims of assault by teenagers like this?"

George answered, "I don't know about that, but our students are closely supervised by trained staff. They are bussed to and from school. They are not allowed to leave the school grounds during the day."

"They will vandalize our homes."

"They are closely supervised. Research indicates

teenagers do not vandalize homes near their school but in their home neighborhood."

"You must build a 12 foot wall around your school."

. "There is a fence around the playground and my students are closely supervised. We do not have the funds to build a 12 foot wall all the way around the school."

"These are dangerous kids, and they should be in jail."

"None of my students have committed any type felony that would require imprisonment. They are troubled youngsters who need help. My staff are with these youngsters all of the time, and they are not afraid of them. There is no reason for you to be frightened." (George didn't tell the group he currently had a student who killed a neighbor with a bow and arrow. The neighbor was attacking the boy's father in their front yard. He was later cleared. The incident was considered self-defense. He was a mild student and seemed to pose no danger.)

George could not convince the neighbors that NEED was safe to have in their neighborhood. The hearing lasted all day. The committee debated for a long time. They finally gave George their decision. He would have 90 days to prove to the neighbors they were safe from his students. If there were any major incidents during the next 90 days between NEED students and neighbors, he would be called before the committee to explain.

He had again doused the dragon's fire.

George advised his staff the neighbors were closely watching them. No student was to leave the playground. Students who voluntarily left campus, or were

excluded for the day, must be followed by a staff member until they cleared the neighborhood. They breezed through the 90-day probationary period with no problems. George felt the city and the neighbors were satisfied. Not true! The next attack on NEED would be more subtle.

Four months had passed since the hearing and everything was going smoothly. The city committee was satisfied. Then one day George walked out of his office to find a strange woman looking at one of the fire extinguishers in the hall. George approached her,

"Hello. May I help you? "

"No, I was just leaving."

She walked out the door and down the steps. He followed her out and watched her go into a house down the street. He was puzzled. He checked the date on the extinguisher and it was current.

Nothing else strange occurred until a week later. Four men with clipboards came to George's office. "Are you Dr. Saiter?"

George could not deny it since his name was on the door. "May I help you?"

The dragon smiled.

They introduced themselves. There was a fire inspector, a building inspector, code inspector, and an electrical inspector. The leader of the group explained, "There has been a complaint signed by a number of neighbors that you are out of city zoning compliance for the use of the building. We are here to inspect your building to see if that is true." They showed George their credentials.

Things began to roll downhill.

George alerted all staff the building was being inspected and to cooperate with the inspectors. They crawled over the building like ants. They went into every room, used stepladders to peer into the ceilings and walls, opened panels, and climbed into the attic through the ceiling. They did the same thing on the outside of the building. Everywhere they went they made notes and checks on their clipboards. They were still inspecting when the students and staff left for the day.

George pulled his chair out into the hall and watched. Finally, they began handing George written notices of noncompliance. Each inspector gave him five or six notices. They thanked him and left.

George nervously thumbed through them. Each notice gave him 30 days to react. A quick estimate of the cost of compliance ranged between 50 thousand and 60 thousand dollars. The neighbors had done their job. He would finally be shut down.

George informed the building owners but they were unwilling to do any upgrading to the building to comply with the notices.

He informed Goodwin. Goodwin's suggestion was, "We will have to shut it down. We can spread the staff out in the BOCES for the balance of this year's contracts." After this time, George rarely talked with his supervisors when he was in trouble because the only answer he seemed to get was, "Shut it down!"

George's first reaction was to give up. Life would be much easier if he just worked as a school psychologist. That thought really looked attractive and seemed to have a lot of merit.

He slowly regained his perspective over the next week. He resolved not to give up without a "good fight." This program is important to the kids, parents, and the whole community. He would fight until the last breath. He did not tell Brown or any of the other staff about the problem. From experience, he knew problems like this upset and frightened the staff and could affect how they did their job.

He made an appointment with the Supervisor of Inspectors (I will call him Ed Harper, a fictitious name). George needed more information. He needed to find out more about the problems and what alternatives, if any, he might have. He had to wait a week to see Harper. He read everything he could on building codes. He still had 20 days. Maybe he could get an extension.

Harper was friendly and sympathetic. He understood what was happening with the neighbors. George asked why it had operated all these years as a business school and now the building was out of compliance for his school. Part of the answer was that we had younger students than the business school. Some of the compliance issues were new. They were new regulations passed two months earlier. George asked him to go over each notice with him. Some were easily resolved, such as the number and placement of fire extinguishers. They sorted out the easy ones from the big ones.

George agreed to immediately take care of eight of the complaints. Ed Harper overruled several other complaints. They ended up with about five that were big money items and could not be easily resolved. They involved firewalls, automatic fire doors, a new roof, and a sprinkler system. Harper gave him a thirty-day extension. That was some relief. They would meet again in a week.

George had no solution for the five items when they met the second time. They talked for several hours. Finally, Harper said, "I disagree with the original inspectors. I will overrule them. I see no safety hazard that would require firewalls and a new roof. Your doors are fine. They are 30-minute doors and meet all codes. None of them need to be automatic. I have talked with my supervisor at length about this. The sprinklers are a problem. However, that regulation was enacted after you received your Certificate of Occupancy. Therefore, you are grandfathered in as far as this code is concerned."

All five problems dissolved with a stroke of a pen.

Harper declared, "I declare you are in compliance with all building codes of Colorado Springs."

A sigh of relief escaped George's lips. He shook Harper's hand and thanked him profusely for his understanding and cooperation. George's feet never touched the pavement as he left the municipal building.

He had killed the dragon. George did not know it, but the dragon was only wounded. He would rear his ugly head many more times during George's love affair with NEED and his troubled students.

The program was running well now. Benusa left the second year and George needed a new head teacher. He had one teacher who often criticized his decisions. He decided to give her a role in decision-making. She was a bright and caring teacher. George promoted Beverly Bailey to head teacher. She developed into an excellent supervisor and became a loyal employee and friend.

The budget was tight and funding continued to be tough. School districts complained about the cost of treatment, but when they had a student they could not control they were glad to call NEED. Colorado Springs District 11 again made up more than half of the placements. Their intensive care unit had not been successful.

It was around Thanksgiving of 1984 when the dragon reared his ugly head again. He was hard to keep down.

Newspaper headlines: **Memorial Hospital Purchases Blair Building To Start A Nursing School!** George had been blindsided. The contract for the Blair building included a 60 day notice to vacate.

He received the notice to vacate on December 1, 1984. He had convinced the neighbors that they were not threatened and solved the inspection threat, but there was no fighting this one. He was looking for a new home or shut it down. Here we go again.

It was a custom of NEED, started by George, to have a Christmas party for all staff and their families. This year's party was difficult for George. After the New Year George would have to tell his staff NEED was closing and they would no longer have jobs. During the party George had trouble interacting with staff due to his heavy heart.

George rigorously scoured Colorado Springs and the surrounding area for a suitable building. He could find nothing that did not have some limitation making them unsuitable. He finally located a building for sale. He thought he was going to put together a deal, but it collapsed at the last moment. It was now the middle of January with no prospects in sight.

Goodwin instructed him to draw up a plan to disband NEED. He was to find a place in the BOCES schools for the staff to complete their yearly contracts. NEED would be no more. The board and superintendents were notified they would need to find alternate placements for their students. The superintendents were not happy but had no solution.

George chose to wait until the last moment to notify staff. He still had hopes. He tried to get an extension from the Blair owners but was turned down. He talked with the hospital to delay the deal to no avail. The last week of January was upon him. He was desperate.

In one last desperate attempt George again called all the real estate agents listed in the phone book. No one had or knew of anything that would fit his needs. After the twenty fifth call, he saw an agent's name in the yellow pages he had never talked with before. Nate (a fictitious name) answered the phone. George went through his story of his need for a building to house a program for troubled students. After listening to George's desperate plea, Nate said,"I may have a possibility. I have a listing for an office building for sale that might work for you. There are only four offices occupied. The owner wants to sell because he has been unable to rent. He is behind on payments and in financial trouble. Let's go talk with him."

Nate picked George up at his office. Ben (fictitious name), the owner, met them at the building that was located on North Academy Boulevard. There was a complex of five buildings with a large parking lot. The north building was a two-story building with wooden siding. It was not pretty but could be functional. The carpets were worn, and the paint was peeling, but the building looked like a "haven in the storm."

George had to make it work! His back was to the wall. The deadline to move was only five days away. Two of the tenants were in the process of moving. The third one had 30 days on their contract and the fourth had a year left on his contract. George negotiated the rent down to where he could afford it.

Ben would get two of the tenants moved out by the end of the week. The others were notified they were to share the building with forty troubled youngsters and given the opportunity to move. Both tenants chose to stay out their contract. George assured them he would try his best to make it comfortable for them.

George triumphantly notified Goodwin of the new building. He agreed to the terms and would take the contract to the board. George could go ahead with the move.

Two borrowed trucks hauled the furniture to their new home. The whole staff, plus some parents, turned out to help move on the last day of January.

What a miserable day to move. **The temperature was 10 degrees below zero.** Every one worked hard. They finished the move late in the day. Staff spent Sunday arranging furniture in the new school and were ready for students Monday morning. Adjustments had been made to accommodate NEED in the new building. He was proud of the staff. The landlord was happy because he now had the whole building rented, and he could make mortgage payments.

The dragon lay seriously injured and bleeding, but he was not done yet.

CHAPTER FIVE

NORTH BUILDING, ACADEMY BLVD

1985 - 1986

NEED had a new home, but they had close neighbors. This did not prove to be a problem this time. The third tenant moved at the end of the month. The last tenant liked kids and enjoyed the NEED students. They now called the program NEED Junior Senior High School. School ran relatively smoothly the rest of the year. There were always incidents with students. They seemed to take turns losing control. Each one was dealt with as it arose. This is, and always was, a high stress program.

Staff had become well stabilized. They were good people who cared for the troubled children and always made that extra effort to help them in spite of the foul language and disruptive behavior.

The end of the year came without major incidents. Two

weeks after the end of school, George received a letter from a municipal judge. The letter cited a complaint made by one of the building owners in the complex. The judicial order gave George 30 days to shut down the program and vacate the building.

Here was the dragon's ugly head again. Would it never end?

George was back on the defensive. This order coincided with a lawn mower accident when George lost the end of his index finger. The surgeon had pulled the skin up over the missing end and secured it by many stitches.

George, with his throbbing bandaged hand in a sling, presented the judicial order to The NEED Foundation Board. Goodwin was chair of the board. Even though George was not paid to work in the summer he spent many summer hours on the job. The board had no solutions to the problem. Again, closing down was the only answer they had. (Not much help.) There was no money to fight the order in court. George told the board his hand was hurting so much he could not think straight. He begged them to give him two weeks before making a final decision. The board voted to grant him the delay and scheduled another meeting in two weeks.

George recuperated at home for several days while he tried to think of a solution. He decided to talk individually with the other building owners in the complex. His first meeting in the campaign was with the owner of his building. He was not even aware of the court order. He was as upset as George because he needed the revenue from NEED to pay his mortgage. He would help in any way he could.

The next meeting was with the building owner adjacent to the complainant. Mark (a fictitious name) was chair of the

Building Owners Association. George's payments helped maintain the commons areas of the complex. Mark was also not aware of the court order nor was he in favor of it. He had no problem with the students. They conversed for several hours to find a way to reverse the order. Mark said the person who filed the complaint was an angry man and was always threatening to sue someone. Mark finally said he would call for a meeting of the Building Owners Association and try to convince him they needed the program in the complex. The meeting was set for the next week. They did not invite George to attend.

Mark promised to call after the meeting and inform him of any solution. The day came for the ten A.M. meeting. George was nervous. The Foundation Board meeting was in two days. Again, for the one hundredth time, (it seemed), NEED was in danger if he failed to present a solution in the next two days. Twelve o'clock came and went without a call. George checked his phone to see if it was still working. He got a steady dial tone. One o'clock – two o'clock – two thirty – the phone rang. George grabbed the phone. Mark assured him all was well. "The court order will be rescinded." NEED was safe again – for a while.

Dragon, you are losing your flame.

During the fall quarter Beverly Bailey, Head Teacher, developed health problems. She began to have severe back pains and decided to have surgery to correct the problem.

While she was in the hospital, her right foot would fall forward when she tried to walk. George went to see her one evening at the hospital on his way to teach a night class at the University of Colorado. While they were talking, she had a grand mal seizure. It was horrifying to see a good friend go through such an episode. That night as he told his class of his experience, he cried. Soon after, Beverly had to resign. She was later diagnosed with MS.

Again, George turned to an employee who frequently questioned his decisions for promotion. He promoted Jane Briggs to Head Teacher. She was a strong, loving teacher with outstanding classroom control skills. She became an excellent supervisor and a loyal employee.

Jane Briggs

The rest of the year went smoothly with no major threats to the program. There was just day-to-day trauma with troubled youngsters and parents. The staff was cohesive and stable. Holes appeared in the walls mysteriously right at the kicking level and doors were found hanging from broken hinges. The building was not built to withstand the wrath of an angry student.

George was tired of making repairs by himself. He decided the program was now strong enough to afford a part time handy man. He put an ad in the paper and began to interview prospects. His first question was, "Can you hang a door?" Then he would ask them to take him through the steps of hanging a door. This stopped several applicants. An older fellow was next to be interviewed. George liked him right away. He answered all the questions in a way that told George he knew what he was doing. George hired Jerry Barusa on the spot. He kept the building in good shape from then on. All the kids and staff liked Jerry.

One day his janitor failed to show up. He had quit without notice. The building had to be cleaned daily so George pitched in to do the job. His sweet secretary, Carol, could not stand to see George cleaning alone, so she stayed overtime to help him, (with no extra pay.) George advertised the next day for a replacement but was unable to fill the job for two weeks. Each night George and Carol cleaned toilets, scrubbed floors, and vacuumed. The third night she brought in her son to help. Then there were three to do the cleaning until a replacement was hired. Carol was one of George's key employees and became a lifetime friend.

Carol Gardner

One afternoon in April a well-dressed man walked into the building and asked if he could talk with the director. George came out of his office and shook hands with him. He identified himself as Fred Sampson (a fictitious name). He was a loan officer for one of the nearby banks. They had just foreclosed on the South Building. He asked George if he was interested in owning his own building. He had just tapped into one of George's favorite dreams. He said he could make him a deal he could not refuse.

George chuckled. "I have no money to make a down payment on your building."

Fred said, "I don't need a down payment."

"I have no funds to pay for a move."

Fred replied, "That could be solved."

George now became interested. Fred offered to show him the building. They walked across the parking lot to see it. George slowly inspected the building room by room. It was a good office building and in much better shape than the one they were now renting, but was not laid out in a way that could be used by the program. George finally said, "I am interested, however it would take $20,000 to remodel so it would meet our needs."

He pushed the banker further.

"Fred, I would need $20,000 to remodel plus $2,000 to move. If you can accept a mortgage large enough to pay off the old loan and give me $22,000 at the closing we may have a deal."

Surprisingly, Fred agreed. It was a good deal for the bank. They would move a foreclosed property. It would be good for NEED if George could pull it off. He had already run the figures, and the mortgage payments would be lower than he was now paying for rent.

There were obstacles. He would need to convince the owner of the North Building to let him out of his lease at the end of the school year. He knew the other building owners would be agreeable because an empty building does not pay into the association for maintenance of the parking lot and grounds. This would decrease their maintenance costs. He knew the BOCES could not take on the mortgage at this time because they were involved in a plan to buy the main BOCES office building.

He went to Goodwin with a plan. He would use the NEED Foundation to buy and own the building. He would then rent the building to the BOCES for the NEED program. The rent would cover the mortgage, utilities, and association fees. Since the rent would be less than they were paying at the North Building, it would be a savings for the districts sending students to NEED. Goodwin wasn't sure if it could be pulled together but was willing to proceed. As an incentive, George would write into the bylaws of the Need Foundation that if the foundation was ever abandoned all assets would go to the BOCES. This seemed to satisfy Goodwin and the superintendents.

The superintendents agreed with his plan, and a week later he got permission from the BOCES governing board to proceed. His next hurdle was breaking the lease where he was now located. He met with the owner. The owner was reluctant to lose his rental income but, as a building association member, he saw the value in getting an owner for the South Building. He would still have rent coming through August and this would allow him time to get new renters. He reluctantly agreed to allow George to break the lease.

George called a meeting of the NEED Foundation Governing Board. He outlined his plan with them and they agreed to proceed.

The closing was in May, 1987. Everything went smoothly. A check was issued to the NEED Foundation for $22,000. The first mortgage payment was due in September. NEED had a new home. George now needed to get the building remodelled and move the program so it would be ready for students in the fall. That did not turn out to be an easy task.

George had been working on the remodelling plans since he first started the process of buying the building. The plans were almost complete. He needed a contractor. Sheila Jobes husband, Rick, is a very talented person. He had just passed his contractor's examination. George gave him his first job. As it turned out it was also Rick's last contractor job. After he finished remodelling the new building for George, he wanted nothing to do with the contracting business.

George went over the plans with Rick and told him it had to be done with $20,000. There was no more money. Rick studied the plans and agreed that he could do it for the $20,000. They were on their way for a bumpy ride. George and Rick got along well throughout the ordeal, even when things fell apart, as they frequently did.

The dragon was again breathing fire.

The first unforeseen problem was the fire alarm system. The city inspector wanted an elaborate fire alarm system and automated doors that would close when the alarm was activated. These doors on both floors would divide the building into segments, therefore containing a fire in segments of the building. All the doors would need to be exchanged for "thirty minute" doors. Supposedly, a fire would take thirty minutes to burn through these doors.

Then they wanted a firewall built in the attic to divide the building in half. This was a tough job because electrical wires passed through this area and each had to be fire proofed. George and Rick conferred each time something came up and would alter the plans to comply and still stay in budget. There were delays on top of delays. A subcontractor would sometimes fail to arrive as scheduled. Rick was getting gray hair, and George was developing ulcers.

The summer wasted away and school time was quickly approaching. The greatest blow came with final inspection.

The inspectors gave him a list of some 25 items that must be done before opening. None of these items had been mentioned before even though they had met a number of times during the summer. Construction funds were running low. There was no money or time to complete the items the inspector now insists must be done. George and Rick were stunned. The project was at a standstill, and the first day of school was ten workdays away!

George needed serious help. His college friend, Wayne Hoeben, was a building inspector for Longmont, Colorado. George talked with Wayne on the phone and explained his problem. Wayne agreed to take a few days off work and come to Colorado Springs.

Wayne looked over the plans, the building, and the inspector's requirements. He said a number of the items were only suggestions in the building code and not requirements. George arranged a meeting with the inspector, his supervisor, Rick, and Wayne. The meeting that took all afternoon got very technical between Wayne and the inspectors, but Wayne knew their language. They slowly whittled away items. There were a few items that Rick said wouldn't cost much. These were conceded to the inspectors.

George began to see a pattern in the arguments. He questioned the inspectors, "Are these big items due to classifying NEED as a school?"

"Of course" the head inspector shot back.

George replied, "NEED is a mental health treatment facility. How does that affect these items?

The head inspector shook his head and said, "They all go away." The road block had dissolved.

The remodel was quickly completed and a Certificate of Occupancy issued by the City of Colorado Springs.

NEED staff flocked in to paint the school rooms and move furniture. They were ready for children in their very own remodelled building on the first day of the school year 1987/88.

NEED finally had a home to call their own!

The dragon was again put to rest.

CHAPTER SIX

SOUTH BUILDING, ACADEMY BLVD

1986 - 1991

They were finally in a building of their own, but problems would continue to surface.

George changed head teachers at the beginning of the year. Jane Briggs and Linda Boles were hired one day apart. He decided to rotate head teachers each year. This is the year Linda would be head teacher. She did a wonderful job. She loved the students, and was a good administrator. She also did an excellent job of relating to sending schools.

Linda Boles

George never made the change back to Jane, and that was

not because she did a poor job. She was a fine Head Teacher. Operations were running smoothly and he did not want to "rock the boat." Jane and Linda continued to be good friends and loyal employees. Jane never held a grudge because of this decision.

In 1988, George reorganized the administrative structure again. He created the position of Assistant Director and bestowed the title on Linda. Jane became Head Teacher again.

He promoted Carol Gardner to Office Manager. She was a hard working employee and deserved everything he could do for her. Bill Brown was still Clinical Director.

George developed an Administrative Committee that would help make program decisions. This committee was made up of his administrative officers. The committee was a success. The administrators worked well together because they all had a voice in operations. Sadly, pay raises did not come with the increased responsibilities. George hoped that would come later.

NEED was now the largest and most profitable BOCES program and provided its major funding.

The fluctuation in student numbers remained a problem. Student population was always lower at the beginning of each school year. Generally there were fewer educational staff also due to resignations at the end of the previous year. He would delay replacing educational staff until student enrollment picked up. There were fewer turnovers with the clinical staff and this could mean he might have to layoff good clinical people until the population increased. This would mean he would lose experienced and established clinicians and then need to train new ones, perhaps only months later. This was an unacceptable situation. He must find a way to fund the positions until they were needed.

After much thought "outside the box," he identified what

he thought was a needed service in the BOCES districts. The small districts could not afford to hire full time social workers to deliver therapy to the few special education students who were identified in staffing. He thought, "What if he could supply the districts with part time therapists for an hour, a half day, or a whole day a week to deliver these services?"

He developed a price schedule that would pay the social worker's salary plus travel costs and presented the idea to Goodwin. This would be a win-win solution. It would fund the surplus treatment staff and provide a needed service to the districts.

Goodwin considered the idea and the price structure. He liked it and said he thought it could work. The superintendent council agreed, and the BOCES board approved the plan without a dissenting vote. "Clinical Outreach" was born. This became a popular program through the years. It was so popular he had to hire extra staff to supply the demand.

Another problem George encountered was the loss of good therapists who quit to start their own practice so he decided to develop an after school program to provide therapy to the general public. This would allow the clinical staff opportunities to have a part-time private practice and still work for NEED.

The NEED Mental Health Center under the NEED Foundation was born. He hired a receptionist and kept the building open until nine o'clock each week night. This did not cause a problem with the BOCES because the Foundation owned the building. The therapists would receive sixty percent of the fees and 40 percent went to pay overhead.

The NEED Foundation Mental Health Center was an excellent source of supplemental funds for extras the budget could not afford. The funds, after expenses, were plowed back into the program and the staff. It paid for billing expenses, Christmas presents, rewards for staff of the month, new furniture for their offices, etc.

George screened walk-in patients. If they could pay, or had insurance that would pay, he passed them on to one of the clinical staff. If they could not afford therapy, or could pay only a small amount, George kept them for himself. He always required them to pay at least $5.00 per session. He was soon working from 7 A.M to 9 P.M. many days.

The NEED program started accepting elementary children in the spring of 1988 due to the demand for services

Karen Wadleigh

from BOCES districts. George hired two excellent teachers for this program Karen Wadleigh, and Cathy Wishart. Wadliegh served as the lead teacher for the elementary program. NEED now served First Grade through 12th grade. Serving elementary students turned out to be even more demanding than secondary.

The following year hail damaged the shake shingle roof enough for the insurance company to offer to replace it.

George obtained bids and awarded the contract. It was mid-April. The snows were over, and they had entered a dry period. A crew removed all the shake shingles and under covering. They lifted new roofing material to the roof and distributed it for application. A one-week delay followed while waiting for the roofing crew. The roof was unprotected.

George was unhappy with this delay. He was soon to

become downright furious. Sunday night produced a late winter storm of twelve inches of wet snow. The snow was melting rapidly in the bright sun by noon on Monday.

There he is again.

The problem first started in the elementary classroom on the second floor. George was summoned by the elementary teachers. Water was dripping through the ceiling in a dozen places. Wadleigh was trying to teach reading while the water dripped on her head and her students. She would move the group to a non-dripping place only to be inundated with new drips. It was funny to look back on, but George could see no humor at the time. Conditions were the same in the other classrooms.

George screamed into the phone when the contractor finally answered. "Do you know what you have done to my school? You have destroyed it."

The contractor agreed he had been negligent but he could do nothing until all the snow had melted. "I will repair everything," he assured George.

"You better get your crew ready because I'm also charging you for every day of school we lose. You'll have to pay my teachers for the extra make up days."

The contractor assured George he would be ready to start repairs the next morning. He moved all the students downstairs to finish the day. He had to shut down school for the next two weeks while the crews replaced carpet, drywall, and ceiling, throughout the two story building. It was a big and terrible mess. It broke George's heart to look at his beautiful school in such a mess.

He hounded the crew every day of the two weeks it took to repair the roof, tear out the walls, floors, ceilings and then restore them. The time was made up at the end of the school year. The contractor's insurance finally paid everything, including the cost of extra school days that George demanded because he wouldn't sign off until he was completely satisfied.

The one continuous problem is, has been, and always will be, funding. The BOCES members accepted the costs as long as George kept them reasonable. The state now took over payment for non-member district children. George would now bill the state monthly for each out of district student and the state would collect from the district. This smoothed out the money flow.

George's job also smoothed out. It had become easy. After 13 years of continual strife, George wasn't used to "easy."

The dragon had skulked back into his cave for a long nap.

The staff was excellent and stable. Outreach was going well. Bill Brown worked as a full time outreach therapist while Dennis McDowell temporarily held down the Clinical Director position. Bill's people skills were excellent. He can be recognized as the one who made "Clinical Outreach" work. George had to hire extra therapists to supply the demand. The Mental Health Clinic was at full capacity.

George decided it was time to move on. He announced his retirement at the end of the 89/90 school year. He would work one more year.

It was a bittersweet time. It was hard to walk away from a program over which he had sweat so much blood. Yet, he thought it was time to go. George had one final bitter pill. The committee to search for his successor did not include him! This really hurt. He had built this program from a dream and nursed it through mighty rough seas. Why couldn't he have a say in his successor? However, the "powers that be" choose otherwise. He could not change that. He didn't necessarily disagree with the committee's choice, but he didn't have a say in the choice.

George and Norma flew into Boston in mid-January of 1991. They were attending a job fair for overseas teachers. They interviewed for Peru, Indonesia, Taiwan, Aruba, Cypress and several other spots around the world. They had several offers but decided on a teacher and counselor job on the island of Aruba for two years. It turned out to be a wonderful experience.

Linda Boles and Jane Briggs put together the greatest retirement party any one could imagine. Present and past staff showed up. All the outside contacts such as probation officers and consultants attended. There were over 100 attendees. Many stood up and gave testimonials about him.

It was a great night. George was moving on. He was headed for the island of Aruba.

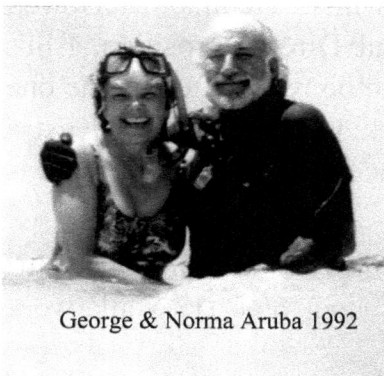

George & Norma Aruba 1992

He never dreamed the program would survive the next forty years, or that it would become the **"George Saiter School of Excellence."**

The End

NEED PROFESSIONAL STAFF WHO MADE A SIGNIFICANT POSITIVE CONTRIBUTION TO CHILDREN

These are the professional staff members George feels made a significant impact on the lives of children, their families, and consequently, on his own life, and the success of his dream. These people had strong personalities, caring hearts and the skills to effectively carry out their jobs.

They did not always agree with George and were strong enough to let him know. He respected their ideas and often changed his mind after listening to their reasoning. Regardless of his decision, they would go back to work and carry on as a team. This is the cream of the crop. George hired many employees during his sixteen years with the BOCES, but these are the ones who made the cut. He chose only the exceptional ones for this group. This list is presented in alphabetical order. George felt a kinship with each of these professionals and count them as good friends.

Bailey, Beverly: Teacher, Head Teacher; good administrator, loyal employee, good PR with families and school districts.

Bast, Kay: Lead Teacher; self-contained classroom, excellent teacher.

Boles, Linda: Teacher, Head Teacher, Assistant Director,; great disciplinarian, excellent PR with school districts and families, soft heart for kids.

Briggs, Jane: Teacher, Educational Coordinator, Head teacher; excellent teacher, has natural ability to handle out of control children, loyal employee.

Brown, Bill: Social Worker, Clinical Director, Outreach Therapist; first hired, exceptional with children and families, always there when I needed him, helped build thew program.

Barusa, Jerry: Handy Man; part time building maintenance, dependable, loved the kids.

Feldman, Steve: Social Worker; good clinician, missed New York City so much had resigned and returned to the Big Apple.

Ferguson, Mary: Nurse; (part-time), dependable, liked the kids and they liked her.

Gardner, Carol: Secretary, Office Manager; special person, extremely loyal, superb manager, lifetime friend.

Graebert, Brian: Neurologist; volunteered his time, provided needed medical, psychiatric services to children and their parents.

Grow, Marilyn: Speech Therapist; (part-time), already working for BOCES when George hired her for NEED, great therapist, very loyal.

Grubb, Susan: Social Worker; hard worker, excellent therapist, took special interest in students and families.

Grubb, Dr. Ted: Psychologist; competent psychologist and therapist, loyal employee.

Hartman, Judy: Art Teacher, great art teacher, handled

unruly students well.

Howells, Peter: Social Worker; worked with staff, outstanding therapist and consultant.

Jobes, Shelia: Teacher; first teacher hired at NEED, outstanding educator, great classroom management.

Kruger, June: Social Worker; first rate therapist,enjoyed her work.

McDowell, Dennis: Social Worker, Clinical Director; kept everyone laughing, excellent therapist and manager.

Meider, Jill: Psychiatric Nurse; kind gentle therapist, loved students, loyal.

Milligan, Kerry: Social Worker; good with students and families.

Nicolas, Dr. George: Psychologist; great team member, fine psychologist and therapist.

Nici, Jane: Teacher; caring competent educator, loyal hard working employee.

Rosenthal, Dr. Roy: Psychiatric Consultant; volunteer, bright, first rate diagnostician.

Roszman, Tom: Social Worker; hard worker, loved his work and the students.

Serby, Debbie: Art Teacher; creative, caring educator, excellent with children.

Shaw, Carol: Art Teacher; remarkable art therapist.

Thies, Karen: Social Worker; made substantial contributions, good with students

Trujillo, Ralph: Building Maintenance; talented carpenter, "kick proofed" our building.

Wadleigh, Karen: Elementary Teacher; superb caring and talented teacher, loved the ornery kids.

Walker, Dr. Steve: Psychologist, Consultant; provided excellent ongoing in-service for our clinical staff.

White, Dr. Chad: Psychologist; intellectual, George took him under his wing, mentored his professional growth, responded well to mentoring, superb diagnostician.

Winn, Harriet: Volunteer; volunteered for five years. It is difficult to find words to describe her effect on NEED. She endeared herself to staff and students.

Harriet Winn

Wishart, Cathy: Elementary Teacher; teamed with Wadleigh, They took the wildest kids, and educated them, and they loved every kid.

Yeagley, Dr. Miles: Psychiatrist,; volunteer, excellent consultant, helped staff, students, and parents.

Zelmanow, Jeff: Attorney; provided pro-bono legal services for NEED. Drew up the papers for NEED Foundation, good friend.

NEED CHRONICLES

Gleaned From Need Archives

All stories are true, only the names are changed to protect their privacy. All girls will be named "MaryA, MaryB, etc." and all boys will be called "BenA, BenB, etc."

Christmas dinner at the Four Seasons Hotel – December 17, 1981

Staff felt the self-contained students should have the experience of fine dining at a four star restaurant so they convinced the Four Seasons Hotel to donate a four course dinner for some of our students.

Five staff members and seven students (six boys and one girl) attended the dinner. The students ranged in age from 14 through 18. None of the students had ever experienced this kind of meal. Staff and I were seated beside each child around one table.

BenA sat on my left side and BenB sat on my right. Both are diamonds in the rough. The matre d' served us our first course of chicken noodle soup. BenB wanted to start as soon as he got his soup. I encouraged him to wait until all had been served. He was really cued in on the crackers in front of his plate. BenC, seated at the head of the table looked at his soup and complained, "I come clear up here for dinner and all I get is soup?" BenB immediately grabbed a pack of crackers and began to munch them down. BenA crumpled a hand full of crackers into his soup. I then demonstrated to both of them how to hold a cracker in their hands and carefully ladle their soup from the front to the back of the bowl. In the meantime, BenB was on his third package of crackers and scooping up his soup in rapid motion. I advised him to slow down. I looked back at BenA. He was bent down about three inches from his bowl slurping and scooping his soup into his mouth. I explained to him how he should sit up straight and slowly eat his soup.

The second course was salad. I told BenB to not eat anymore crackers since he had downed a half dozen packages already. BenA was complaining that he didn't like cherry tomatoes and mushrooms. He was pulling them out of his salad with his fingers and piling them on the table. I told him not to touch his food with his fingers, but to push them aside with his fork. BenD, across the table said, "I don't want to say anything but eating all those crackers is gross!" I looked back around at BenB and there was a whole pile of cracker wrappers in front of him. He had scarfed down six more packages of crackers. I moved the crackers so he couldn't reach them. Coca Cola was then served to everyone. Both of my boys gulped all of theirs down before I could stop them.

Our main course was chicken breasts with hollandaise sauce and mushrooms, mixed vegetables, and sautéed potatoes.

MaryA announced to all she was eating "chicken tits."

Ben began eating European style with knife in right hand and fork in left hand. I chose to allow this. I kept after both of them to slow down. BenA held up a mushroom that had been on his chicken and ate it, "Hamburger, its good." I said, "I thought you didn't like mushrooms?" "Is that a mushroom?" and started throwing them off his plate with his hand. "Do not touch your food with your hands!" He replied, "That yellow stuff on my chicken is yuck," and started scraping it off on to the table.

The matre d' informed us dessert would be mousse. Several of the kids piped up, "Meat for dessert?" All staff assured the kids mousse is a pudding. BenA loved it. After I admonished BenB to eat slowly. I turned to find BenA had finished his mousse and was licking out the bottom of the bowl. Several of the kids didn't like theirs but BenB leaped to the rescue. He devoured all that was offered to him. BenD, a senior, organized everyone for a picture.

I took out a $20 bill for a tip but was reluctant to leave it on the table until all kids were gone. BenE saw the $20 and asked if that was a tip. He said, "I'll handle that." I reluctantly handed it to him. He took the money, held his arm out to MaryA who took his arm very lady like and they walked down the stairs together. The matre d' and his waitress were standing at the bottom of the stairs shaking hands with the children as they left. BenE with MaryA on his arm walked up to the matre d' in a very suave manner, shook his hand, and said, '"Thank you sir, for the very fine dinner and excellent service. Here is a little something for your fine service." BenE and MaryA smiled sweetly and walked out. I stood there amazed. This is the same boy who came into our program completely out of control, who upset tables, broke windows, and busted doors.

BOYFRIEND

MaryB came to school extremely upset. She sat and cried and could do no work. Her teacher finally got her calmed down enough to tell her what was wrong. MaryB blubbered, "My boyfriend is leaving for the army." Teacher, "I didn't know you had a boyfriend. Where did you meet him?" "At the bus stop this morning!"

BROKEN BICYCLE

We devised a work-study program for BenK. He is to

come to school for half a day then go to work for a business that rents out video game machines. He receives $2.00 per hour. He likes his job so much he wanted to leave school early. We needed to be firm that he wait until a certain time to go to work. He brought his bike to school today so he could get to work faster, (rather than ride the city bus.) I made him keep the bike in my office. When it was time to leave Brown took him to my office to get his bike. He rushed into my office to find his front tire was flat. There was a little slash mark on the side of the tire that both he and Brown could see.

BenK flew into a rage screaming, "They slashed my tire." In a burst of anger, he grabbed his bike threw it down the hall. He ran after it, picked it up, raised it over his head, and slammed it to the floor. Brown was trying frantically to calm him down. He urged him to go outside so he wouldn't disturb the other students. BenK grabbed the bike, rushed out the door and threw it on the ground with great force. He then kicked it over into the weeds and started jumping up and down on it. All the while screaming, "They slashed my tire."

Brown finally got him calmed down enough to look carefully at the front tire. The slash mark they saw was not cut all the way through. It was an old cut with dirt in it. Brown finally convinced him the tire had not been slashed. It must have just gone down on its own.

BenK just stood there panting looking at his bike. He cried, "Oh, s—t look at my bike." The spokes were broken. A pedal was gone, the handle bars were bent, it was junk. He started crying and trying to pick up the pieces of the broken bike. He blubbered, "How am I going to get to work now?" Brown loaded the sobbing boy into his car and took him to work. I guess he will be riding the city bus to work for a while.

THE ESCAPE

BenG was a likable kid. We all liked him, but he was very difficult. He was arrested one day at school for theft. He allegedly loaded up a pickup at a guest ranch near town with saddles and anything else he could find and drove off. While he was in detention he feigned an injured leg (late at night) from playing volley ball. They finally decided it was serious and secured a judge's order to take him to the hospital for an x-ray. The x-ray tech said he couldn't x-ray him with the chains on his legs. The guards removed his leg irons and also all his clothes except his shirt and under pants. He was put on the table, and the x-ray machine was set up. Everyone had to leave the room during the x-ray. BenG decided that was a good idea. He would also leave. He escaped out of a window into 25 degree weather clad only in his under pants and a shirt. He was gone for two days before turning himself in.

PLAN MISFIRED

BenH was an eleventh grade student in our self-contained classroom. He was difficult to motivate but was very happy when he was cooking in our lunch program. Kay Bast, our self-contained teacher, had developed a lunch program for the class. A couple of students were selected each day to cook lunch and clean up afterward. It was very popular with the students. BenH did a great job cooking.

His therapist arranged for him to learn to cook Chinese food in a Chinese restaurant as a future profession. He would work three days a week as an apprentice to become a Chinese cook. However, workman's compensation insurance was a problem, the restaurant owner, who was doing us a favor, refused to buy the insurance. I got our vocational rehab person to put BenH in the rehab program and pay the insurance cost. They also picked up his salary since the restaurant would not pay him. Pay was a requirement of the insurance. This took a lot of staff time and effort to arrange.

Everything was finally put in place. BenH had not been told of the negotiations because we didn't want to disappoint him if it fell through. His parents were excited about the possibilities.

His therapist sat down with him to tell him the good news. After she completed telling him all the details, BenH said, "Chinese food makes me sick. I can't stand the sight of it." His therapist came into my office requesting permission to "kill him!" Another of our great plans bit the dust.

STRANGE PARENTS

BenJ related a troubling story to his social worker. He said he was riding in the car, with his dad and mother. All three were arguing when his dad got so angry he drove the car off the road, through a ditch and into a tree. He backed the car up at high speed and banged into another tree. He then put the car in drive, gunned the motor into another tree. He continued banging into trees, swearing all the time, throwing the three of them wildly around inside the car, until he practically demolished his automobile.

He also said when his dad gets angry with him he threatens to pull him out of NEED or make him stay home for a day. It is interesting that the parents see him liking the program so much they can use his attendance as a tool to threaten him.

WILD BUS LOADING

I was informed of problems during bus loading after school. There was fighting, yelling, and screaming, resulting in angry bus drivers. I decided to observe the problem. It was a riot. Students would come running out of the building and get on the bus. They would sit for a moment, jump off the bus, and run back into the building. Some would jump off the bus, light a cigarette and try to get back on the bus with the cigarette. The bus driver would then order them to get rid of the cigarette or get off. Some would comply but others defied the driver until she kicked them off the bus.

There was a steady string of students jumping off the bus and running to and from the school getting sodas or just to be contrary.

The drivers would get frustrated and threaten to drive away and leave students. This was ironic because we fought all day long to keep students in school and when school was over we couldn't get rid of them.

I decided we would lock the doors after school so the students couldn't get back in after they left. This caused a lot of additional anger in the students who would stand banging on the doors to get in. Finally they all accepted it and things settled down after school.

DEAD BUG

BenK came to school one day with a friend. BenK was reminded he could not bring visitors unless he got permission in advance. His friend would have to leave. Forty-five minutes later, I was informed BenK had become unruly and asked to leave school for the day. I called his mother and informed her BenK was excluded from school for the day.

About an hour later I noticed a strange car drive by my window. (The Rocky Mountain Rehab building had a driveway surrounding the building.) It looked like BenK driving the car. I dismissed the thought because I knew BenK was not old enough to drive. A short time later a different car buzzed by my window. Again it looked vaguely like BenK at the wheel. After the third incident, my head teacher came into my office and informed me BenK was driving around the school in different cars and giving our students the finger. I called his mother again to inform her of the latest escapade of her son. She was extremely upset with her son.

The pattern was to circle the school two times and then leave. George found out later that BenK had convinced a used car salesman he was going to buy a car. In good faith, the salesman let BenK and his friend try out several cars. His friend had a driver's license.

The fourth time BenK drove past my window I rushed outside to waylay him on his second round. As I waited, I heard a tremendous crash on the other side of the building. I rushed around the building to find BenK's borrowed car sitting on top of a vintage VW bug in the landlord's parking lot! When BenK came around the parking lot, he floored the accelerator to "peel out." The gas pedal stuck, he lost control of the car and fish tailed out into the street. He jumped the curb, careened across the lawn and into the RMR employee parking lot. The speeding car then broadsided a vintage VW bug ramming it into the car parked beside it and ending up on top of the heap. He had destroyed three cars, the borrowed car, the VW, and the car next to the VW. I would have to deal with my landlord later and try to placate several extremely angry people.

I helped BenK and his friend out of the car. Neither of them was injured. I took them to my office and called the police and then his mother. Her first comment was, "I will kill him." I told her she would have to wait in line. BenK was charged with driving without a license and reckless driving. His parents would have to pay for all three cars. This caused extreme family tension, to say the least.

IN THE NAVY

One of our former students, BenI, rode into our parking lot on a motorcycle. BenI graduated from NEED two years earlier after being with us for two years. He had an explosive temper and quit school at least a dozen times. We managed to hang onto him until he graduated. His last two months prior to graduation were horrendous. His behavior escalated as he neared graduation, and he realized we would not be around to help him anymore. When he graduated his face was filled with pride in his accomplishment. NEED staff was pleased also.

With his diploma in hand he joined the Navy. However, he had to clear up one problem with the law before they would accept him. He had stolen an Army vehicle which constituted a federal offense. The charge was dropped depending on how he performed in the Navy.

During boot camp he got fed up with the high discipline and went AWOL. He quickly reconsidered and returned to camp. He completed boot camp and is now assigned to an aircraft carrier as a plane captain. He is in charge of launching aircraft. His rank is E-3.

He acted very mature during his visit. He visited all his old teachers and social workers and thanked them for helping him through school. It is a great feeling to see his success knowing how difficult it was for him and our staff.

CARING EDUCATORS MAKE A DIFFERENCE

When our daughter was 4 years old (now she is 17), my wife and I discovered she had many "learning disabilities" stemming from birth defects. Since then we have spent a fortune in psychotherapists, doctors, and various specialists in a effort to help her life be as normal as possible.

During our daughter's years in the Woodland Park School system it was, to put it mildly, pure hell for all concerned. The school was not equipped to handle her problems, and even fought us when we pulled her out of school during the 1980/81 school year and sent her to West Junior High in Colorado Springs.(this was no cost to Woodland Park but personally cost us approximately $1600.) Though our daughter's problems were not solved, it did give her a year's break from the Woodland Park system.

However, by this school year we encountered a new school principal. He is a warm hearted professional, genuinely concerned man. Focusing on our daughters' problems he worked with us to get our daughter placed in a special school in Colorado Springs called "NEED."

Under the extremely capable and highly professional guidance of Dr. George Saiter, and the highly trained staff of the entire school, not only has our daughter been given a new lease on life but so have her parents. Our daughter has gone from one not able to cope with the handicap and report cards of Ds and Fs, to a highly motivated student whose last report card showed all As except one C. Thanks to her teacher, Mrs. Kay Bast, our daughter will begin work this summer at the Easter Seal Handicap Camp.

On behalf of my wife and daughter, I want to thank all of you for turning a very dismal picture into a very bright future. We three are forever indebted to you.

Bill C. Duck, Divide

The Very End

First Thirteen Years